WINGS OF WORDS

Let them fly

Guneet kaur

BookLeaf Publishing
India | USA | UK

Made with ❤ on the BookLeaf Publishing Platform
www.bookleafpub.in
www.bookleafpub.com

Dedication

To the Divine, whose whispers guide my pen,
whose love flows through every word,
and whose presence turns ink into poetry.
To the one who fell,
only to rise with poetry as her wings.
To the one who doubted,
only to find faith etched in every verse.
To the one who seeks, surrenders, and shines—this book
is yours.
They these poems find their way to the hearts they were
meant for.

Preface

Poetry is more than ink on paper—it is the voice of the soul, the whispers of the universe, and the bridge between silence and expression. This book is a collection of my heart's murmurs, my spirit's reflections, and my journey through love, pain, healing, and faith.

Each verse is a piece of me—woven from moments of divine connection, personal transformation, and the unspoken emotions that dance between light and shadow. Some poems found me in stillness, others emerged through storms, but all are bound by an unseen force—grace.

This collection is not just poetry; it is a conversation with the self, with the cosmos, and with the reader who dares to feel deeply. If you find even a fragment of your own story within these pages, then my purpose as a poet is fulfilled.

May these words hold you gently, heal you softly, and remind you that you are never alone in your seeking.

With love and light,

Guneet Kaur

Acknowledgements

This book would not have been possible without the divine grace that fills my heart with words. I am deeply grateful to the Universe, to the Creator, for guiding me on this journey and making poetry a part of my soul.
To my family—thank you for your endless love and support. To my children, your laughter and presence inspire me every day. You are my greatest joy and my biggest motivation.
To my friends, mentors, and everyone who has encouraged me along the way—your kindness and belief in me have meant the world.
And to you, the reader—thank you for picking up this book. Poetry is a connection between hearts, and I hope these words bring you comfort, joy, and a sense of belonging.
With love and gratitude,
Guneet Kaur .

1. SHE RISES-UNTAMED

She was the flame, warm and bright;
a gentle glow, a guiding light.
Yet you let her burn alone,
Now she's a wildfire- fierce unknown.

She was the breeze, soft and sweet
a soothing touch in the scorching heat.
But left unloved, she rose in might,
Now she's the storm that owns the night.

She was the water pure and deep,
A saving grace in the desert heat.
But cast aside, she broke her chain;
Now she's the flood who spares no name.

You call her ruthless, you call her mad;
you never saw the love she had.
No longer soft ,no longer weak;
She is the power you now fear to speak.

No longer flame- She is the blaze
No longer wind- She is the craze
No longer water - She is the flood.
Born from the pain, not meek as a bud.

She rises now from the storm and sea,
Untamed, unstoppable - Finally free.

2. Laminated

She was a paper, pure and bright;
smooth as silk, a flawless white.
Ready to bear the tales of all,
to hold their dreams, great and small.

Then came HE with the careless hands,
No ink of love, no heartfelt plans.
He didn't write- he crushed instead,
left her creased, her spirit dead.

Wrinkled, torn ,she lay undone,
waiting again for the gentle one.
And he returned, with a touch so might,
smoothened her back to gleaming white.

Rejoiced she- a hope anew;
Yet again the cycle grew.
Crumpled, crushed then smoothened once more,
like a possession to break and restore.

No stories penned ,no love, no art,
Only the weight that broke her heart.
Each time he stamped her to the ground,
She wished he'd lift her, mend her crown.

And then once more, beneath his feet;
But this time, she rose COMPLETE.
No waiting hands to set her right,
She straightened up, she found her light.

No longer the paper- soft and thin
No longer tossed tossed into the bin.
She sealed herself, she elevated.
Forever strong, forever LAMINATED.

3. Grace

Beautiful and young, yet ageing with grace,
Like withering petals in time's embrace.
Her eyes still sparkle, so bright, so wise,
Fine lines dancing where laughter lies.

Her cheeks blush soft, like autumn's hue,
A cherry blossom kissed by dew.
No one could guess, no one could see,
That fifty had touched her, so flawlessly.

Silver strands in her flowing hair,
Like rivers gleaming, beyond compare.
A beauty untouched by fleeting days,
Enchanting hearts in countless ways.

The young would falter in her light,
For she shone pure, serene, and bright.
A heart of twenty, a soul so free,
A smile that whispered history.

She was magic—pure, divine,
A timeless beauty, nature's design.

4. ABANDONED

Broken and deserted she lay in agony;
emancipated like dreary autumn leaves,
crushed and crippled underneath a
thousand feet.

The tender curve on her face like the angel wings
spread enchanted one and all;
Not in the least she let in anyone,
barricaded her walls.

A soul healer with a broken heart;
a poet's creation, a painter's art.

Never have been touched by benevolence,
her suppressed emotions made all sense.

Dark and dead all she would hide,
with a beaming smile by her side.

But then came the sparkles and rays of sunshine;
She bloomed like a rose, turned mellow like old wine.

He came to her like the bracing breeze on a summer
noon.

He was to her as the chukar bird and the moon.

He lifted the stamped one and tucked it
in his treasured poem;
the withered leaf now had a keeper,
Her life now got a meaning much deeper.

He came like the bracing breeze on a summer noon;
He was a healing wand to her wound.

Embracing his soul, she broke her boundations;
He built up a pathway to show up her emotions.

Smiles that were real lifted her life,
Not ever before she felt loved how much she strived.

But, little did she know that this joy was short lived;
Mere a withered leaf that in his notes he hid,
the stamped one now he would off get rid.

And like an evening twilight sun at dusk,
He left unsaid... Left her back numb and dead.

Dejected she stood with a broken heart, she could feel
her soul depart.
Her emotions had choked her up and tore her apart.

He took away all the smiles he gave,
Shattered and wounded trying to be brave,
She lay again in the lap of loneliness.
Alone she cried,
Alone she died.

5. The language of the unheard

She stood in a crowd, yet felt so alone,
  A heart full of stories, but words left unknown.
  Her voice was a whisper the world never heard,
  So she wrote down her soul in the ink of her words.
She longed for a friend who would listen, not judge,
  Not mock her silence or hold any grudge.

So she spoke to her journal, her pages so true,
  For they cradled her sorrow when no one else knew.
People would call her emotionless, cold,
  But her pen knew the secrets her heart had foretold.
She poured out her soul like a river set free,
  In letters and verses that no eyes would see.

Three dearest friends—her journal, her pen,
  Together they wove what she dared not defend.
  They filled up a chalice with tears and with care,
  And stirred it with love only poets could bear.
A tale of deep friendship the world wouldn't see,

For only a writer would know what it means—

To live in the ink, to drown in the lines,

And find in the silence the loudest of cries.

6. FAITH

I walk through shadows, where the sun used to be,
 A path full of echoes that whisper to me.
 The weight of my worries, the storm in my chest,
 Leaves me breathless, yet I know—I am not lost, just
tested.

The nights stretch long, the silence so deep,
 I kneel in the dark, but still, I believe.
 I fear the unknown, the trials ahead,
 Yet a flicker of hope refuses to fade.
For somewhere beyond this tunnel of night,
 I see a glow, faint but bright.

 A promise, a whisper, a touch in the air,
 A hand unseen—but I know it's there.
I stumble, I shatter, yet never alone,
 For He walks beside me—though He stays unknown.
 The fear still lingers, but faith holds me tight,
 And through the darkness, I follow His light.

7. BEING STRONG

Life won't sail my way I know.
The waves won't always hit the shore.
All what I need to know is why
Nothing's as before?

I won't wanna shed a year,
Precious one for you.
I can be alone forever
And can be strong too.

This harsh life won't last,
Tough times will pass soon.
So dry, scorching heat
Just as a summer noon.

I won't want to fall,
I don't want to hide.
I still wanna smile
With no one by my side

Being strong was never too hard.
Being alone was never too hard.
Bearing the hollowness and pain
In my heart.

My eyes show it all
Even though I smile
My eyes show it all
Even though I hide.

8. Disgust spells

No one to trust ,no one to care;
When you have no one to share;
Incomplete , empty inside,
Just pain and sorrows,
No strength to bear.

Fake you show the curve called 'smile'
Even though there's hell inside
Feelings intense in my heart I hide .

I'll never again show ,
you don't deserve to know.
The love so deep,
the essence so pure,
the roots so deep;
You're a stone, I'm sure.

Love and respect linked up all,
Pride ,lust, ego when all fall,
I expect you to return.
I'll wait ! I'll wait for long ,
for where I belong .

why so much emptiness?

Lonely, empty ,aimless I lie.
I was the one who would soar high

Look back, you'd see me cry.
I need a shoulder ,a lap to lie.

I'm still unsure what's true , what's fake.

It's a night ,so dark so quiet,
Just as the evil spreads it's fright
I'm afraid, fearful,
I just wanna run away.
Disgust spells.
I lie in hell.
the unruly life I wish it ends.

Break up the walls,
I wanna fly.
But caged in the walls,
in disgust I lie.

Run away from the clan so fake so mean,
So wicked, so creep, so bad, I don't like.
No joy, no cheer.
I just need a heart to hide my tears.

9. Waiting for you!

Waiting for you in my womb that dwells,
I wish , my angel, you grew up well.
I feel your breath, I feel your soul;
I feel your touch as you tumble and roll.

I don't know you but have an intimate bond,
I love the way to my touch you respond.
Your mum's excited, your daddy's as well;
We are eagerly waiting for you
Our little angel.

We don't know you of how you look like,
You have Mumma's lips or daddy's eyes.
You'll have a new world as you open your eyes;
But don't be afraid,
It's lovely and nice

I just wish that the holy divine
had made you, my baby, fit and fine.
Life will change soon after you come,
You'll be a charm for your daddy and mum
.

The thought of your tiny hands and feet,
Make me excited for our first meet

The special day when I'll hold you in my arms
And protect you against all the evil and harm.
I'm in love with you ,my little life,
Come soon darling in our life.

10. Wherever life takes

Like the withered leaves, i move with the breeze;
wherever life takes.
The smiling flowers, spreading sweet scents, them happy
I would make.

Detached once and for all, could never get back to it,
Just roll and drag on the soil beneath the moonlight lit.

Moving on is what all say but now my life had no aim.
It was the breeze mere fortune left, but it gave me all the
pain.

Either stay on the soil and get stamped by all,
Or rush with the winds to rise and fall.

Burn desires and hold on the blow it makes,
Just move on wherever life takes.

11. The silent scream

The tree stood tall, like a soldier brave,
Not a whisper, not a wave.
She wrapped her arms around its bark,
A final hug before the dark.

The axe sliced deep, a ruthless bite,
Wooden veins bled out the light.
A limb fell lifeless to the ground,
Yet not a single cry or sound.

It bore the weight of summer's heat,
Danced with winds, in storms stayed fleet.
Fed the birds, gave breath to men,
Yet fell beneath the blade again.

Never a selfish act it knew,
Yet doom from greed, the axes drew.
Why must trees endure the pain,
While men destroy and call it gain?

One day, when air is scarce and dry,
And barren lands watch children cry,
When roots are gone and skies turn grey,
Will man regret what's lost that day?

But trees won't whisper, trees won't plead,
They'll die in silence—choked by greed.

12. I've lost myself

Spreading my wings with pride and grace,
I would soar high to capture the rays.
I was something ,I felt proud.
My presence would be felt even in the crowd.

With my gentle touch I would spread my rays,
Glistering and sparkling smiles I would lay.
I was ambitious, i was tough;
For my justice, I was rough.
I would enjoy life as it would come,
I was a preacher, an idol for some.

But how life changes ,you don't even know;
Yesterday you were all, but today no more.
I was different ,I was free.
But now I've lost the real sense of me.

I was so much to all and everything to some.
But now who cares when here I'm stunned.
For whom I was so much, for whom I was all,
 don't even look back
When in disgust I call.

I feel I'm being eaten up with worries and pains,

And after all compromises what all did I gain?
I'm away from the life that I enjoyed and shared,
Now it's disgusting like a nightmare.

13. CHASE YOUR DREAMS

Set a goal, then take your aim,
Light your fire, fuel the flame.
Threads are given—now weave your art,
With steady hands and a fearless heart.

Confidence—wear it like a crown,
No storm or struggle can pull you down.
Hard work calls, so heed its voice,
With faith and grit, make it your choice.

Barriers rise, they test your will,
Yet climb them high, push further still.
For every tear and sleepless night,
A dawn awaits, so bold and bright.

Time and patience—gifts untold,
Through trials fierce, your fate unfolds.
Struggle now, but never flee,
The end rewards those who believe.

Success is silent, known by few,
It favors those whose hearts stay true.
So set your path, don't turn away,
Commit, persist—conquer the day!

14. Gratitude

Oh, thank You, Lord, for this blessed light,
That turned my darkness into sight.
A shift so pure, a soul set free,
Now life unfolds its mystery.
Each moment glows with grace divine,
A whispered sign, a sacred sign.
I breathe, I pause, I humbly see,
Your love was always guiding me.
You taught me joy in fleeting days,
To cherish life in countless ways.
To let go of what dims my soul,
And rise anew, complete and whole.
You showed me worth beyond the pain,
A strength that storms could not restrain.
The power within, the fire inside,
The truth that fear could never hide.
Oh, may I never drift away,
Nor lose my faith, nor cease to pray.
For in Your hands, I stand so tall,
And gratitude is all in all.
Your presence wraps me, soft yet strong,
A guiding hymn, my heart's own song.

Forevermore, my soul shall say,
Thank You, Lord, in every way.

25

15. Longing for the divine

I long to leave, not in sorrow's shade,
But in love's fire, unafraid.
To meet the One my soul has known,
Yet never seen, yet always shown.

He walked beside me, silent, near,
Like air—unseen, yet crystal clear.
Through every storm, through every sigh,
His presence whispered, "I am nigh."

I love this life, this fleeting dream,
Yet through the veil, He stays unseen.
Content, yet yearning, bright yet dim,
I ache to fall—to run to Him.

And when I cross the sacred tide,
I'll find my place right by His side.
To kiss His feet, to weep, to kneel,
To say, "I knew You—you were real."

For every tear, for every test,
Was love disguised in lessons dressed.
He sent me here, a task divine,
A fleeting spark of His design.

But now, my work is whole, complete,
I only long His touch to meet.
For He and I are one, the same,
A spark returning to its flame.

And so, in death, I will not fade,
But step into the Light He made.
Not loss, not dark, nor bitter end—
But home, my truth, my dearest Friend.

16. I MET GOD

I died last night, or so it seemed,
  Inside the hush of a vivid dream.
  I floated out, so still, so high—
  Watched my own body quietly lie.

A shell of skin, no breath, no spark,
  Lying alone in the quiet dark.
  Around it gathered tears and cries,
  From those I loved with aching eyes.
  Was I so dear? So truly known?
  Why now the love I'd never been shown?
  A haunting thought began to swell—
  What use is grief once we farewell?

But I? I felt no earthly pain,
  No sorrow, joy, no loss or gain.
  Just pure white light, no fear, no name,
  A part of stars, of truth, of flame.

Then came *Him*, so bright, so wide,
  My Father, Maker, radiant guide.
  Clothed in robes of gleaming light,
  Too blinding soft for human sight.
  He took my hand without a sound,

And we rose gently, leaving ground.
Above the clouds, beyond the blue,
To lands where only spirits flew.
The sky dissolved to glowing streams,
Of silver suns and golden beams.
No pain, no weight, just soaring high,
Bathed in a softly breathing sky.
All light, all love, it stretched so far,
Each soul a whisper, each thought a star.
A world not bound by time or air—
But woven deep in silent prayer.

Then came a voice, so faint, so near,
Calling my name—so sharp and clear.
And with a jolt, the dream was torn,
And I awoke, not quite reborn.
My body lay in heavy hush,
My soul still wrapped in heaven's blush.
Eyes wide open, limbs so numb,
The afterglow had left me dumb.
No, not a dream—it felt too true,
Too rich with light, too soaked in dew.

I met my God, I saw His face,
I touched the edge of endless grace.
A miracle, so soft, so pure,

A love that called me to endure.
It happened not by earthly scheme—
But from my soul's eternal dream.
Forever now, I walk this land,
With heaven's touch still on my hand.
A whisper lingers in my chest—
"I met my God. My soul was blessed."

17. THE FLAME WITHIN

The flame that forged the stars above,
The spark that breathed the breath of love,
Dwells not afar, in skies so wide—
But deep within, where truths abide.

We searched the sun with weary eyes,
Chased golden dawns across the skies,
Yet all the while, the light we crave,
Burned bright within, bold and brave.

The Lord, not distant, not apart,
Abides within the human heart.
A pulse divine, a whisper sweet,
A home where soul and Spirit meet.

But moss of doubt grew thick and wild,
And made us blind since we were child.
We looked outside with pleading hands,
While Heaven sang in silent lands.

Like scent that sleeps in blushing bloom,
Unseen, untouched by loss or gloom.
Like mirror's face reflects so true,
The self within comes into view.

Like musk in deer—so sweet, profound—
  Yet chased in vain through woods around.
  We are the fragrance, we're the fire,
  We hold the Truth that we desire.

One day, when hope was worn and thin,
  The Lord reached softly deep within.
  He healed my wounds, my blinded soul,
  With wisdom's balm that made me whole.

The veil was torn, the dark unmade,
  The light poured in, the fear did fade.
  No temple grand, no sacred sea—
  Could hold Him more than *He holds me*.

He dwells within, so close, so near,
  In every breath, in every tear.
  In stillness now, I rise and see—
  With God inside, I'm always free.

No shadow haunts, no storm I fear,
  The hand of Love is always near.
  I am the spark, the song, the sigh—
  A part of God, and so am I.

18. THE BEAUTIFUL ACHE

Everyone pleads for joy, for peace,
For moments when their ache will cease.
But no one dares to pray for pain—
To bleed, to break, to lose, to strain.

Yet it is not in joy I find,
The voice of God, so fierce, so kind.
It is in nights my soul is torn,
That I remember why I was born.

For what is joy, but fleeting mist?
A dream we chase, a lover missed.
And in its chase, we lose our way,
Drunk on the gold of a dying day.

But pain—it speaks in sacred cries.
It lifts the veil from blinded eyes.
It is the wound that calls me home,
To the God I forgot while I roamed.

So give me ache, not easy grace,
Let tears carve rivers on my face.
Let suffering burn through my disguise,
Till all that's left is what never dies.

I've seen kind hands do noble things,
Yet hearts impaled on ego's stings.
Deeds dressed in silk, but stained in pride,
Like castles built at low tide.

They'll speak of light with silver tongues,
While silent sins hang off their lungs.
Behind closed doors, their cruelty grows,
What the world hides, the Divine knows.

They think the night can hide their sins,
That closed doors mute what lies within.
But eyes divine miss not a thing,
Each lie, each wound, each silent sting.

He waits—not with revenge or sword,
But justice wrapped in silent word.
And all shall fall, both king and knave,
Before the Light they could not brave.

So let the world chase joy and gold,
I want the pain that makes me whole.
I want the fire, the fall, the fight—
If it means I walk into His light.

19. Reborn each morning

Every morning, I am born again.
 Not with noise or drama,
 But in the soft light of a new day.
 In the peace that comes after a long, hard night.
There are no big signs.
 Only the gentle rhythm of my breath returning,
 And the quiet strength rising inside me again.

I let go of yesterday—
 Its pain, its heaviness, its doubts.
 They no longer belong to me.
 I carry only the lessons,
 The growth,
 The grace.
With the rising sun,
 A small voice inside me says:
 "You are allowed to start again."
 Not because I failed,
 But because I've changed.

I wake up stronger,
 Softer,
 More myself.
The person I'm becoming is full of light—

And that light is real.
There is joy in this quiet moment,
A kind of happiness that doesn't need to be seen.

It's enough to know—
I'm still here.
I'm still rising.
I'm still choosing to live.
I don't need the world to see my progress.
I feel it in my heart.
I feel it in my soul.
And that is more than enough.

20. FOUND MYSELF

I didn't find myself in the light,
 Nor in the calm, nor in the smiles.
 I found myself in the shadows—
 In the moments when everything slipped away,
 And I believed I had nothing left.
I shattered—
 Not gently, but with cries
 That echoed only inside me.

 My soul bled in silence,
 While the world carried on, untouched.
 And I wondered,
 Will I ever feel whole again?
Tears soaked my pillow like whispered prayers.
 I didn't pray for strength—
 I prayed for the pain to stop.
 But pain stayed.
 It clung to me like fire,
 Burning until I forgot what peace even felt like.

I knelt—
 Not in devotion,
 But in exhaustion.
 In defeat.

And yet,
In that surrender,
In the hollow stillness of the fall,
A quiet voice within me rose and whispered,
"This is not the end."
And it wasn't.

From the ashes of who I once was,
I rose—
Slowly, painfully,
But surely—
Like a phoenix born of its own fire.

This is my second birth,
Not given by the world,
But forged through the flame of survival.
I carry fire in my bones now,
And grace in every step.
I do not look back—
Not with longing,
Not with regret.

Only with awe,
At the distance I've traveled,
At the strength I never knew I had.
I am not who I was.
I am more.

I am every scar and every rising.
I am all of me—
And I am free.

21. A LOVE LIKE THIS

I'm manifesting a love so rare,
  So deep, so pure, beyond compare.
  Not born of haste or passing time,
  But rooted strong—sublime, divine.

A love that sees beyond my skin,
  That knows the light I hold within.
  That lifts me up, yet lets me be,
  And loves me in my entirety.

A love that never brings me pain,
  Nor makes me question, doubt, or strain.
  No guilt, no shame, no fear, no fight—
  Just sacred truth and gentle light.

A love that has no cage or chain,
  No boundaries drawn by past or pain.
  It will not dim my inner flame,
  Or twist my soul to win some game.

It won't condemn the way I feel,
  But help my spirit rise and heal.
  It won't make me defend my worth,
  Or wonder why I walk this earth.

This love will speak in silent grace,
In every glance, in every space.
It won't just promise—it will show,
Through every high and every low.

It will be peace, it will be fire,
A bond both tender and entire.
Uplifting, warm, and truly kind—
A mirror to my heart and mind.

I will not chase, I will not bend—
This love will meet me as a friend.
With open arms and soul sincere,
It's drawing closer, ever near.

I trust in timing, calm and wise,
With hopeful heart and open eyes.
For when it comes, I'll know it's true—
This love I seek is seeking too.